Life on a Coral Reef

TEXT BY MARY JO RHODES AND DAVID HALL
PHOTOGRAPHS BY DAVID HALL

Undersea Encounters

Children's Press®
A Division of Scholastic Inc.
New York Toronto London Auckland Sydney
Mexico City New Delhi Hong Kong
Danbury, Connecticut

Library of Congress Cataloging-in-Publication Data

Rhodes, Mary Jo, 1957–
    Life on a coral reef / Mary Jo Rhodes and David Hall; photographs by David Hall.
        p. cm. (Undersea encounters)
    Includes index.
    ISBN-10: 0-516-24395-0 (lib. bdg.)   0-516-25463-4 (pbk.)
    ISBN-13: 978-0-516-24395-5 (lib. bdg.)   978-0-516-25463-0 (pbk.)
    1. Coral reef biology—Juvenile literature. 2. Coral reef ecology—Juvenile literature. I.
Hall, David, 1943 Oct. 2– II. Title.
    QH95.8.R48 2006
    577.7'89—dc22

                    2006002322

*To our editor Pam Rosenberg, who showed unbelievable patience with
my seemingly endless list of "just one more" changes.
—D.H.
To my son Jeremy, whose early interest in science and nature brought out
the scientist in me and helped to inspire this series.
—M.J.R.*

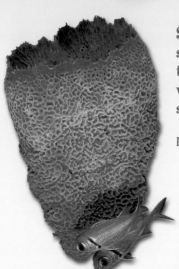

Sponges are the simplest animals that can be seen without a microscope.
pg. 22

Life on a Coral Reef

Angelfish are among the most colorful fish found on coral reefs.
pg. 21

This hawkfish is waiting to pounce on a small fish or shrimp.
pg. 10

A grouper rests beside a yellow sea fan on a coral reef in Papua New Guinea.

chapter 1

What Is a Coral Reef?

Warm seas are home to a group of animals that look like plants. They are small, but they have built some of the largest structures on Earth. These animals are corals, and the structures they build are coral reefs.

Coral reefs help shelter coastlines from the fury of storms. They provide food for millions of people around the world. And coral reefs are home to more kinds of animals than any other place in the ocean.

mouth

tentacles with stingers

Some of these coral polyps are hiding inside their limestone homes, while others are completely visible.

What Are Corals?

Corals, or **coral polyps**, are small animals about the size of a fingernail. Each polyp has a mouth leading to a stomach. The mouth is surrounded by many tentacles that are covered with stingers.

Most coral polyps live together in large groups called **colonies**. Within a colony, each polyp builds a small "house" to protect itself. The colony grows larger as new houses are built on top of older ones.

Hard Corals

Some corals build reefs and some do not. The polyps of reef-building corals, or hard corals, have a multiple of six tentacles. They make their homes out of limestone, using calcium found in seawater. Working together, hard coral polyps build large, rocky structures.

Divers swim over a reef of hard table corals in Indonesia.

What Do Corals Eat?

A coral polyp uses its stinging tentacles to capture **zooplankton**, small animals floating in sea water. But this alone does not provide enough food for reef-building polyps.

Living inside each polyp are microscopic plants called **algae**. These simple plants use sunlight to make food for themselves and their coral partners.

Hard coral polyps can have many tentacles. The number of tentacles is always a multiple of six, such as twelve, eighteen, or twenty-four.

The polyps of this coral colony are scattered along its white limestone skeleton.

How Does a Coral Colony Begin?

A colony begins with a young coral animal called a **larva**. The larva attaches itself to the seafloor and develops into a polyp. The polyp grows and later divides to become two polyps. The two divide again to become four, and so on. Eventually, there may be thousands of polyps in the colony.

Coral Reefs

Each new generation of coral polyps builds its homes on top of the limestone skeletons of the

Coral reefs can be seen in the shallow water surrounding these small islands in the tropical Pacific Ocean.

previous generation. In this way, hard coral colonies grow larger. Over time, the colonies grow together to form large structures called reefs. The largest coral reefs are thousands of years old.

Hard corals and colorful soft corals provide shelter for many reef animals.

Soft Corals and Sea Fans

Soft corals have a flexible skeleton that can bend without breaking. There are many kinds of soft coral, including sea fans, sea whips, and tree corals. Soft coral polyps have eight tentacles with many side branches. They don't build reefs, but they do provide homes for many reef animals.

Great Barrier Reef Fact
One of the largest structures on Earth is the Great Barrier Reef of Australia. It is more than 1,250 miles (2,012 kilometers) long.

9

A freckled hawkfish rests on a
hard coral branch, waiting to
pounce on a small fish or shrimp.

chapter 2

Living with Coral

Corals provide food and shelter for many fish and **invertebrates**. Some animals just live on the coral colonies, while others eat the polyps. Many fish hide from **predators** among coral branches. Predators also lurk among the branches. Animals that live with coral are often difficult to see. They may change color to blend in with the coral on which they live.

The feathery antennae of a Christmas tree worm are used to capture bits of food floating in the water.

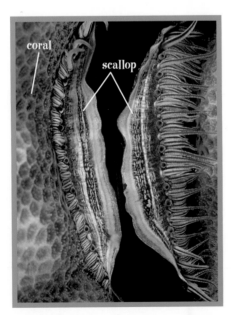

coral

scallop

Coral scallops live inside holes in hard coral.

Living in Coral

Christmas tree worms live in hard coral. The worm hides inside a hole, with two feathery antennae sticking out. The antennae trap bits of food floating in the water. This method of obtaining food is called **filter feeding**. To protect itself, the worm can instantly withdraw its antennae, closing the entrance to its hole.

Another filter feeder that lives in hard coral is the coral scallop. The coral grows around a young scallop, creating the hole in which the scallop lives. Scallops have rows of tiny eyes that sense light and movement. At the first sign of danger, the scallop closes its shell tightly to protect itself.

Living on Coral

Gobies are among the smallest of all vertebrates, or animals with backbones. They are tiny fish that often live on the surface of corals. Many gobies are colored to blend in with their coral partners. Some coral gobies have bodies that you can see through.

Gobies are small fish that live with many kinds of coral: brain coral (left), soft coral (middle), and wire coral (right).

Among the Branches

Some animals live among the branches of hard corals, where predators cannot reach them. Among these are tiny coral crabs. Young damselfish swim near the coral and dart into the coral branches at the first sign of danger.

A Coral Disguise

There are many hidden animals on a coral reef. Some hide by disguising themselves to look like coral. The slender filefish can take on a color pattern that resembles a branching sea fan. The trumpetfish floats head down, blending in with nearby whip corals. The tiny pygmy seahorse has red bumps on its body that resemble the polyps of the coral on which it lives.

Some fish are disguised to look like coral: a filefish with a sea fan (top), a pygmy seahorse with soft coral (middle), and a trumpetfish with gorgonian coral (bottom).

Coral as Food

Some fish and invertebrates eat coral polyps. Most of them do no serious damage to the coral, which soon grows back. Fish that eat coral polyps include filefish and butter-flyfish.

Cowries are snails that eat coral polyps. Their flesh-covered shells make them look like coral, which helps to hide them from predators. Some of these snails even have fleshy growths that stick out from their bodies and resemble polyps.

A pair of small filefish feed on branching hard coral. Their long snout helps them reach inside the small limestone cup where each polyp is hiding.

Cowries are snails that may eat soft corals. Each kind of cowry typically resembles the coral on which it lives.

15

This coral reef in Fiji provides food and shelter for a school of damselfish.

chapter 3

Coral Reef Fish

Coral reefs are home to some of the most colorful fish in the world. The bright colors often communicate messages to other fish on the reef. For example, they help some fish to keep track of their mates or to find new mates. Some fish have bright colors that warn rivals to stay away from their territory.

Bright colors can also help to protect a fish. They may create a pattern that is confusing to predators. Other color patterns may warn predators that a fish is poisonous or has a powerful sting.

Wrasses and Parrotfish

Wrasses and parrotfish are closely related coral reef fish. Most of them mature first as females and later become more colorful males.

Parrotfish eat mostly algae that grow on or in corals. Their teeth are fused together to form a beak like a parrot's. The beak is used for biting off chunks of coral. Wrasses are predators that eat snails, crabs, and other invertebrates.

A parrotfish uses its strong jaws to bite off a chunk of coral. A small wrasse is waiting to make a meal of any animal frightened out of hiding.

Damselfish come in many different colors. They hide among coral branches when a predator approaches.

Damselfish and Clownfish

Damselfish may be small, but they are fierce fighters. They will defend their territory against much larger fish. Some damselfish eat algae, while others feed on drifting zooplankton.

The most colorful members of this family are the clownfish. They live with stinging **sea anemones** for protection from predators.

Surgeonfish have sharp, defensive spines to discourage predators.

Surgeonfish: Grazing on Plants

Surgeonfish are plant eaters that graze on the algae growing on rocks or dead coral. They are named for the sharp spines located near their tails. These scalpel-like spines are used for defense against predators. Most surgeonfish swim in large groups known as schools.

Groupers are predators that eat small fish and crustaceans.

Groupers and Basslets: Large and Small Predators

Groupers are among the largest predators on coral reefs. Most of them catch and eat smaller fish and **crustaceans**. Basslets are related to groupers, but are much smaller. They swim together as a harem—a group in which there are many females and just one male.

Butterflyfish and Angelfish: Butterflies of the Reef

Butterflyfish are among the most colorful fish on the reef. They often have a dark bar through their eyes and, sometimes, an eyespot near their tails. This color pattern can fool a predator into attacking the tail end of the fish. This makes it easier for the butterflyfish to escape being eaten.

Angelfish are equally colorful and are close relatives of butterflyfish. They are usually larger, often about 12 inches (30 centimeters). They differ from butterflyfish because they have sharp cheek spines. Young angelfish often have a very different color pattern from adult angelfish.

To confuse predators, many butterflyfish have an eyespot near their tail. Their real eye is usually disguised by a dark, vertical band.

There are more than seventy **species** of angelfish. Most of them are found only on coral reefs.

Coral Reef Invertebrates

Invertebrates are animals that have no backbone. There are more different invertebrate groups found on coral reefs than anywhere else on Earth. These groups include **mollusks**, crustaceans, **echinoderms**, **sponges**, and **sea squirts**.

Sponges are the simplest animals that can be seen without a microscope. They have no nerves or muscles and cannot move at all. All sponges are filter feeders.

Nudibranchs are colorful mollusks related to snails. They are predators that feed on corals, sea anemones, sea squirts, and sponges.

This blue sea star and its relatives are echinoderms, or "spiny-skinned" animals. Other members of the group are sea urchins, sea cucumbers, brittle stars, and feather stars.

These tiny shrimps are living on a sea cucumber. Shrimps, crabs, and lobsters are crustaceans. Crustaceans have a body with three sections, a hard outer skeleton, and legs that bend at joints.

Adult sea squirts, also called tunicates, look a bit like sponges, but don't be fooled. They are the most advanced of the invertebrates. Their swimming larvae have the beginnings of a backbone.

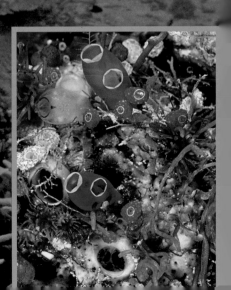

A female reef squid attaches her eggs to a dead tree branch that has fallen into the water. Her mate stands guard to prevent another male from fertilizing her eggs.

chapter 4

New Life on a Coral Reef

New life can be found everywhere on a coral reef. Coral colonies grow as new coral animals are formed asexually. Asexual reproduction occurs when a coral polyp divides in half to become two animals. Each of these new animals is an exact copy of its only parent.

Corals can also reproduce sexually by releasing eggs and **sperm** into the water. When a sperm and egg unite, a

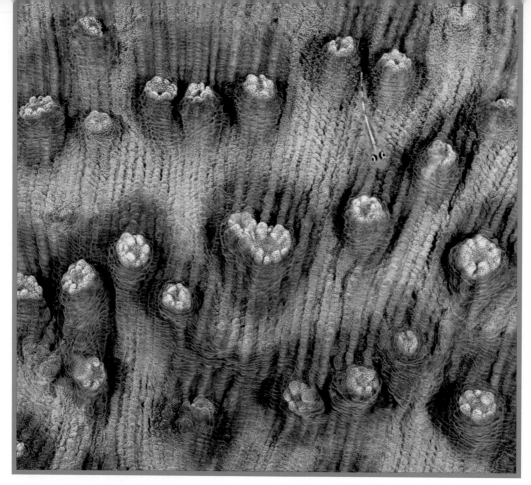

The coral polyp in the center is dividing to become two polyps.

new animal is created. If the sperm and egg come from different colonies, the new animal will have two parents. It will not be an exact copy of either parent. The new animal soon develops into a coral larva. The larva may drift for many miles before attaching to the bottom and starting a new colony.

This coral colony is about to release pink bundles of eggs and sperm into the water.

Male and Female at the Same Time

Corals are not the only animals that produce eggs and sperm at the same time. When two nudibranchs mate, each one supplies sperm to fertilize the other's eggs. After mating, both animals lay eggs.

These nudibranchs are both male and female. After they mate, both will lay eggs.

27

A male basslet keeps a harem of several females. When he dies, one of those females becomes a male and takes his place.

Fish That Change Sex

When necessary, a male clownfish can change sex and become a female. Parrotfish, wrasses, groupers, and basslets do the same, but in reverse: they mature first as females and later become males. A male basslet has a harem of many females. When the male dies, the largest female will change sex in order to take his place.

Fish Egg Fact

Coral reef fish can lay thousands of eggs, but only a few survive to become adults. Most of the eggs are eaten by other fish and filter-feeding invertebrates.

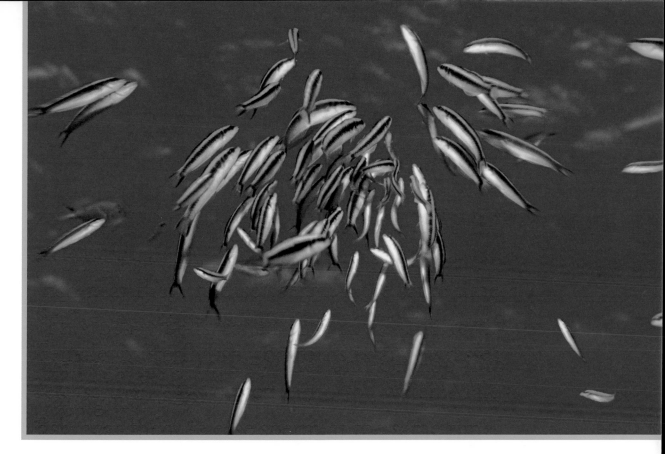

One female is accompanied by many male wrasses during spawning. When she releases her eggs into the water, the males release their sperm.

Scattering Eggs in the Water

Female butterflyfish, parrotfish, and wrasses release their eggs directly into the water. Male fish near them release sperm at the same time. This behavior is called spawning. The fertilized eggs float in the water and develop into young fish.

Guarding the Eggs

A female clownfish lays her eggs on a rock near her sea anemone. The male fertilizes and guards them. At first, the eggs are bright orange, but after just a few days you can see the baby fish inside each one.

The bright orange eggs gradually darken as the baby clownfish grow. The eyes of the developing fish are visible inside each egg.

Using a Nest

Female gobies and damselfish prefer to place their eggs in a nest. Male damselfish clean the surface of a rock, creating a nest where the female can lay her eggs. Some female gobies lay their eggs on coral branches. The male goby fertilizes them as they are being laid. He then guards the eggs for five or six days, until they hatch.

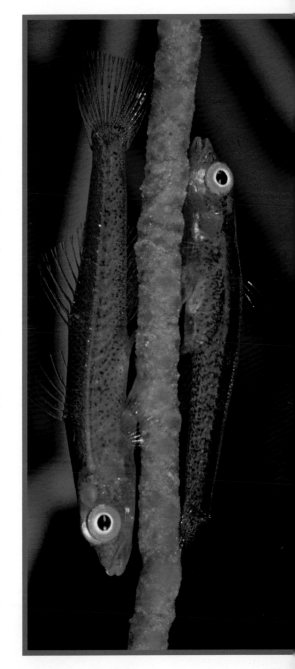

A female goby (right) deposits her eggs on a coral branch and her mate fertilizes them. The tiny eggs cover the coral branch, giving it a bumpy appearance.

Soldierfish are out on the reef at night, but they seek shelter inside caves during the day.

chapter 5

The Coral Reef at Night

Depending on the time of your visit, a coral reef can seem like two different places. During the day, you will see many colorful fish and other animals going about their business. But at night, most of these daytime fish are asleep. After dark, a different group of animals takes over the reef.

Corals in Hiding

During daylight hours, most hard coral polyps hide inside their limestone

Hard coral polyps remain inside their limestone homes during the day (left). At night they emerge, extend their tentacles into the water, and begin feeding (right).

houses. You can see only the hard skeleton. At night, when coral-eating fish have gone to sleep, the polyps come out of hiding. They extend their tentacles and begin to feed on zooplankton.

The Night Patrol

Like corals, many crustaceans are **nocturnal** animals. They hide in holes during the day, so that fish won't eat them. At night, most shrimps, lobsters, and crabs come out to search for food.

A Hunter with Eight Arms

The octopus hides in its den by day and hunts at night. It uses its eight arms to feel its way in the dark. This clever animal can change its shape to fit into almost any crack or crevice in the reef. When the octopus finds a crab, it traps the **prey** in the webbing between its arms.

A reef octopus traps crabs or other prey in the webbing between its arms. The prey is quickly overpowered by the poison that enters its body when the octopus bites.

A Hunter with Sharp Teeth

Armed with needle-sharp teeth, a moray eel is the most feared nocturnal hunter on the coral reef. Morays prey on fish, crabs, and lobsters. Even an octopus may end up in the stomach of a moray eel.

Moray eels are fearsome predators, and octopuses are among their favorite prey.

A pufferfish (left) and a parrotfish sleep at night. Parrotfish secrete a mucus "cocoon" around themselves to hide their scent from nighttime predators.

Day Fish and Night Fish

Many daytime fish sleep in coral caves and crevices at night. Nocturnal fish hide in caves during the day and come out only at night. Cardinalfish, squirrelfish, and soldierfish have extra large eyes, for seeing in dim light. These fish hunt at night for small crustaceans.

The Stars Come Out at Night

Many sea star relatives make their appearance after dark. Delicate brittle stars (right) come out of hiding from under rocks and inside sponges. Basket stars, which are curled up into a tight ball during the day, open up at night. The yellow-brown basket star below is holding onto coral. It has spread its long, branching arms wide to form a giant net for filter feeding.

This Caribbean coral reef appears healthy, but most Caribbean reefs have been damaged or destroyed by pollution, overfishing, and coral bleaching.

chapter 6

Coral Reefs in Danger

Most coral reefs are in trouble. They face a growing number of threats. Some of these threats are natural, and some are caused by people. Many reefs have already died or been badly damaged. In time, coral reefs can recover from natural disasters such as hurricanes. But coral reefs don't always recover from damage caused by human activities. Problems caused by people appear to be increasing, and this has scientists concerned.

The crown-of-thorns sea star kills and eats coral polyps. It leaves behind the white limestone skeleton of the dead colony.

Coral Predators

The crown-of-thorns is a large sea star. It has ten to twenty arms and is covered with long, sharp spines. The crown-of-thorns is a coral predator that always seems hungry. It releases chemicals from its stomach that kill and digest coral polyps. A group of these sea stars can cause extensive damage to a coral reef.

Coral Bleaching

Hard corals like warm water, but sometimes the water becomes *too* warm. When this happens, the coral polyps lose their algae and the colony

Ocean Temperature Fact

In some parts of the world, increased ocean temperatures followed by coral bleaching have resulted in the death of more than three-fourths of the coral reefs.

turns white. This is called coral bleaching, and it can cause the death of an entire colony. Severe damage to many coral reefs has occurred in recent years and may be the result of global warming.

Most of the hard corals on this reef in Fiji were killed when the ocean water became too warm.

It has become common to see large areas of dead coral covered over with algae. Few animals can live in these damaged habitats.

The star coral on the left is healthy. The polyps on the right have lost their color due to bleaching.

41

A fish trap rests on a coral reef.

Pollution

Cutting down forests and building homes near the seashore can cause problems. The increased runoff of soil can smother corals near shore. Sewage and harmful chemicals can also wash into the ocean, poisoning corals and other animals.

Harmful Fishing

In some places, fish traps made of wood and wire have caught and killed most of the reef fish. In other places, underwater dynamite explosions used to stun and catch fish have destroyed large sections of coral reef.

Aquarium and restaurant fish are often captured using cyanide, a poison that kills corals. Overfishing has resulted in the decline of many coral reef species such as giant clams, Napoleon wrasses, and some large groupers.

Cyanide is sometimes released into the water to stun fish, such as this Napoleon wrasse. The fish is worth a lot of money in some Asian restaurants, but the cyanide used to capture the fish also poisons the coral reef.

Protecting Coral Reefs

Many coral reefs around the world are being killed by human activities. If we do not stop these harmful activities, most of the word's coral reefs could be destroyed within the next few decades. When we protect coral reefs, we also protect the many thousands of species of animals that depend on them for food and shelter.

Glossary

algae (**AL-jee**) simple plants; some, such as the ones that live inside corals, are tiny; others, called seaweeds, are much larger *(pg. 7)*

colonies (**CAHL-o-neez**) groups of similar animals living together *(pg. 6)*

coral polyps (**CORE-uhl PAH-lips**) small, stinging animals that live in colonies; some kinds, called hard corals, construct coral reefs *(pg. 6)*

crustaceans (**cruhs-TAY-shunz**) animals, such as crabs and lobsters, with an outer skeleton, jointed legs, and two pairs of antennae, or feelers *(pg. 20)*

echinoderms (**ee-KY-no-derms**) spiny-skinned invertebrates including sea stars, brittle stars, basket stars, sea urchins, and sea cucumbers *(pg. 22)*

filter feeding (**FIL-ter FEED-ing**) obtaining food by removing tiny animals, plants, and other small particles from seawater *(pg. 12)*

invertebrates (**in-VER-tuh-brayts**) animals without backbones; invertebrates include sponges, corals, worms, snails, sea stars, and crabs *(pg. 11)*

larva (**LAR-vuh**) a young animal that is very different from an adult *(pg. 8)*

mollusks (**MOL-lusks**) soft-bodied invertebrates that often have hard shells, such as snails, scallops, clams, octopuses, and squids *(pg. 22)*

nocturnal (**nahk-TER-nuhl**) active at night *(pg. 34)*

nudibranchs (**NOO-duh-branks**) mollusks similar to snails, but without the shell *(pg. 22)*

predators (**PRED-uh-turz**) animals that hunt and kill other animals for food *(pg. 11)*

prey (**PRAY**) an animal that is hunted and killed for food *(pg. 35)*

sea anemones (**SEE uh-NEM-uh-nez**) stinging animals related to coral polyps but larger; anemones do not usually live in colonies *(pg. 19)*

sea squirts (**SEE SKWIRTS**) advanced invertebrate animals, with swimming larvae that have a primitive backbone; also called tunicates *(pg. 22)*

species (**SPEE-sees**) a particular kind of animal or plant *(pg. 21)*

sperm (**SPURM**) cells produced by a male animal that can fertilize eggs produced by a female *(pg. 25)*

sponges (**SPUHNJ-ez**) simple animals with no organs, muscles, nerves, digestive tract, or skeleton *(pg. 22)*

zooplankton (**ZO-uh-plank-tun**) small animals that drift with ocean currents *(pg. 7)*

Learn More About Life on a Coral Reef

Books

Cole, Melissa, and Brandon Cole. *Coral Reefs*. San Diego: Blackbirch Press, 2004.

Rhodes, Mary Jo, and David Hall. *Partners in the Sea*. Danbury, Conn.: Children's Press, 2005.

Rhodes, Mary Jo, and David Hall. *Predators of the Sea*. Danbury, Conn.: Children's Press, 2006.

Rhodes, Mary Jo, and David Hall. *Survival Secrets of Sea Animals*. Danbury, Conn.: Children's Press, 2006.

Books for Older Readers

Cerullo, Mary M., and Jeffrey L. Rotman. *Coral Reef—A City That Never Sleeps*. New York: Cobblehill Books, 1996.

Tackett, Denise N., and L. Tackett. *Reef Life*. Neptune, N.J.: TFH Publications, 2002.

Magazine

Kaufman, Les, and Tim Laman, "Color: A Fish's-Eye View," *National Geographic*, May 2005.

Web Sites

NOAA (National Oceanic and Atmospheric Administration) National Ocean Service Education: Corals
(http://www.oceanservice.noaa.gov/education/kits/corals/welcome.html)

Sea and Sky: Reef Life
(http://www.seasky.org/reeflife/sea2.html)

Index

About the Authors

With degrees in zoology and medicine, **David Hall** has worked for the past twenty-five years as both a wildlife photojournalist and a physician. His articles and photographs have appeared in hundreds of calendars, books, and magazines, including *National Geographic, Smithsonian, Natural History*, and *Ranger Rick*. His underwater images have won many major awards, including Nature's Best, BBC Wildlife Photographer of the Year, and Festival Mondial de l'Image Sous-Marine. To see more of David's work, visit www.seaphotos.com.

Mary Jo Rhodes received her master's degree in library service from Columbia University and was a librarian for the Brooklyn Public Library. She later worked for ten years in children's book publishing in New York City. Mary Jo lives with her husband, John Rounds, and teenage sons, Jeremy and Tim, in Hoboken, New Jersey. To learn more about Mary Jo Rhodes and her books, visit www.maryjorhodes.com.

About the Consultants

Karen Gowlett-Holmes is an expert on the classification of marine invertebrates. She has worked as Collection Manager of Marine Invertebrates for the South Australia Museum and for the Australian scientific research organization, CSIRO. Karen has published more than forty scientific papers.

Gene Helfman is an expert on the behavior and ecology of fishes. He is a professor of ecology at the University of Georgia where he teaches ichthyology and conservation biology. Gene is author of more than fifty scientific papers and first author of the widely used textbook *The Diversity of Fishes*.